Published by One Miracle

© Copyright 1992 by Gene Skaggs Jr.

All Rights Reserved

Printed in the United States of America

First Edition, 1992

Portions Reprinted by Permission from "A Course in Miracles"

© Copyright 1975, Foundation for Inner Peace Inc.

ISBN 0-9633394-0-0

ABBREVIATIONS:

The alpha codes adjacent to Page Number References are as follows:

ACIM = *A Course in Miracles*

"T" =   Taken from *A Course in Miracles* Text

"WB" =   Taken from *A Course in Miracles* Workbook

"MT" =   Taken from *A Course in Miracles* Manual for Teachers

"SE" =   Second Edition of *A Course in Miracles*

TABLE OF CONTENTS

TABLE OF CONTENTS CONT'D

A COURSE IN MIRACLES

INDEX OF SYNONYMS

NOTE: Key to listed synonyms = "*" means "SEE"

Act (*EFFECT)
Action (*EFFECT)
All (*GOD)
Ancient Friend (*JESUS)
Anger (*ATTACK)
Answer (*HOLY SPIRIT)
Anti-Christ (*EGO; *IDOLS)
Atonement (*FORGIVENESS)

Beginning (*GOD)
Behavior level (*EFFECT)
Bridge (*FORGIVENESS)

CAUSE (*GOD)
Christ Vision (*EXTENSION)
Cloud bank (*GUILT)
Comforter (*HOLY SPIRIT)
Communciation link (*HOLY SPIRIT)
Communication medium (*BODY)
Condition (*CAUSE)
Consequence (*EFFECT)
Content (*CAUSE)
Correction (*HOLY SPIRIT)
Correct perception (*FORGIVENESS)
Create (*GOD)

Dark clouds (*GUILT)
Delusion (*SEPARATION)
Displacement (*PROJECT)
Dissociation (*SEPARATION)
Division (*SEPARATION)

Effect (*FORM)
Ego's temple (*BODY)
Ends (*EFFECT)
Engine of destruction (*BODY)
Error (*SIN)v
Eternal Guest (*HOLY SPIRIT)

v

FOREWORD

I have been a student of *A Course in Miracles* since 1979 and have been teaching it since 1988. In my initial study of the *Course*, I found that I had great difficulty understanding its content because of the fact that I was applying my old, traditional definitions to the words that I read in the book. This natural tendency made understanding the concepts presented in the *Course* quite difficult, if not impossible. I realized quite early in my reading that *A Course in Miracles* really has a unique language all its own. As I began to understand that language, and the true meaning of the words, I was then able to begin to comprehend the concepts embodied in the *Course* as a whole.

In my work, I also noticed that the *Course* uses many words interchangeably or synonymously. In recognition of this fact, I have listed these companion words in my book following the pertinent words from the *Course*. I wish to emphasize the fact that my book is not meant to be a substitute for the *Course* itself, but is merely intended to aid the reader in studying the principles upon which the *Course* is based.

It is appropriate that I acknowledge the contributions of those individuals without whose help this book could not have been completed. First, I would like to thank First Church Unity, Nashville, Tennessee, Reverend Jimmy Scott and Reverend Patricia Reiter for allowing me to facilitate *A Course in Miracles* Class there. Also, the secretary of First Church Unity, Ms. Betty Dye, is due a special thanks for both her countless hours of typing and meaningful inspiration in my writing of this much needed work. At the same time, I wish to thank Ms. Jeni Hyde for preparing the cover artwork and Mr. Mel Hacker for preparing the final, camera-ready text from which the book was printed.

In addition, I wish to extend my thanks to Ms. Frances Calgy, Ms. Venorice Caudill, Mrs. Charo Hacker, Ms. Louise Howell and Mr. Jason Skaggs for their valuable assistance in my writing of this book. It is my hope that our collective efforts will be found to be of significant value by all students of *A Course in Miracles*.

Gene Skaggs, Jr.
Nashville,Tennessee
February, 1992

1

ABUNDANCE

Abundance is God's premise and it differs from the ego's belief in scarcity. In our oneness with God, we already have everything, since we are one with Him. Can God be lacking in anything?

The trouble with our understanding about abundance is that we don't recognize it. The *Course* states we are already perfect. This radiant Light that is deep within is what makes us complete.

Guilt is what prevents us from recognizing our abundance. This is a course in removing guilt, and by this process we will be reawakened to the abundance of God's Love.

Let me point out that abundance, used in the above definition, has nothing to do with things at the *effect* level.

ACIM Reference to ABUNDANCE

Pg. 56T (Pg. 62T SE) - "In your own mind, though denied by the ego, is the declaration of your release. *God has given you everything.*"

ANGELS

The *Course* is not referring to angels in the same way orthodox Christianity defines angels. Angels are the extension or reflection of love and light of God that is always with us.

ACIM References to ANGELS

Pg. 390T (Pg. 419T SE) - "Your newborn purpose is nursed by angels, cherished by the Holy Spirit and protected by God Himself. It needs not your protection; it is *yours*. For it is deathless, and within it lies the end of death."

Pg. 522T (Pg. 562T SE) - "Around you angels hover lovingly, to keep away all darkened thoughts of sin, and keep the light where it has entered in. Your footprints lighten up the world, for where you walk forgiveness gladly goes with you."

Pg. 334WB (Pg. 342WB SE) -"God's Name cannot be heard without response, nor said without an echo in the mind that calls you to remember. Say His Name, and you invite the angels to surround the ground on which you stand, and sing to you as they spread out their wings to keep you safe, and shelter you from every worldly thought that would intrude upon your holiness."

ATTACK: Anger, Harm

Attack is the attempt to justify the projection of guilt onto others. This demonstrates that they have sinned, and their punishment is justified.

Accordingly, when we project our guilt onto someone, we believe we no longer retain it. The ego says, "Look, you no longer have your guilt, but your brother has it now." What the ego doesn't tell us is that by projecting (giving) our guilt we reinforce it.

Remember, wherever we think our guilt is, that's where we will try to remove it. So if we think our brother has sinned, we will have to attack him. After attacking him, we will have to build a defense, because we feel he will attack in return.

Level One is the belief God will attack us for separating from Him.

ACIM References to ATTACK

Pg. 84T (Pg. 91T SE) - "The relationship of anger to attack is obvious, but the relationship of anger to fear is not always so apparent. Anger always involves projection of separation, which must ultimately be accepted as one's own responsibility, rather than being blamed on others. Anger cannot occur unless you believe that you have been attacked, that your attack is justified in return, and that you are in no way responsible for it. Given these three wholly irrational premises, the equally irrational conclusion that a brother is worthy of attack rather than of love must follow. What can be expected from insane premises except an insane conclusion? The way to undo an insane conclusion is to consider the sanity of the premises on which it rests. You cannot *be* attacked, attack *has* no justification, and you *are* responsible for what you believe."

Pg. 45MT (Pg. 47MT SE) - "Anger but screeches, 'Guilt is real!' Reality is blotted out as this insane belief is taken as replacement for God's Word. The body's eyes now 'see'; its ears alone can 'hear'."

ATONEMENT: Forgiveness, Salvation

The Atonement process occurred the instant the belief in separation crept into our mind. This process of undoing the separation will be finished when every separated Son has completed his part, which is total forgiveness.

In forgiveness, we forgive as much as we can. After this process (forgiveness) we experience peace for a duration of time. Now we are ready to learn more lessons and remove more guilt usually buried "subconsciously".

In the Atonement principle, we have forgiven completely and therefore realize our oneness with our brother and God. It could be said that Atonement is Level One, and forgiveness is Level Two.

Atonement does not mean at-one-ment, as in some new thought movements. It also doesn't refer to atoning for one's sins.

ACIM References to ATONEMENT

Pg. 2T (Pg. 2T SE) - "Miracles are part of an interlocking chain of forgiveness which, when completed, is the Atonement."

Pg. 17T (Pg. 20T SE) - "The Atonement is the final lesson. Learning itself, like the classrooms in which it occurs, is temporary. The ability to learn has no value when change is no longer necessary. The eternally creative have nothing to learn."

Pg. 19T (Pg. 23T SE) - "Our emphasis is now on healing. The miracle is the means, the Atonement is the principle, and healing is the result."

Pg. 75T (Pg. 81T SE) - "The Atonement must be understood as a pure act of sharing."

Pg. 555T (Pg. 598T SE) - "Accepting the Atonement for yourself means not to give support to someone's dream of sickness and of death."

Pg. 46MT (Pg. 48MT SE) - "The sole responsibility of God's teacher is to accept the Atonement for himself. Atonement means correction, or the undoing of errors. When this has been accomplished, the teacher of God becomes a miracle worker by definition."

5

ACIM References to ATONEMENT Cont'd

Pg. 53MT (Pg. 55MT SE) - "Healing and Atonement are not related; they are identical."

Pg. 73MT (Pg. 77MT SE) - "It is concerned only with Atonement, or the correction of perception. The means of the Atonement is forgiveness."

<u>BODY</u>: Ego's temple, Learning device, Hero,
Unmindful, Communication medium,
Engine of destruction, Home of madness

The body came into existence when the thought of separation entered the Son of God. This thought had to be projected outward. This thought, being projected, created the world and body.

From the ego's view, the body is its home and is used for specialness and separation, as well as for proof that the body can't be of God. The ego also states that the body is the cause of pleasure and pain, thereby making the mind the *effect*.

Much like everything in this world, the Holy Spirit gives the body another function. The body is neutral, neither good nor bad, sick nor well. It is the mind that is sick, or the mind that is healed. That is why the *Course* is so adamant about bringing the problem back to its source, which is in the mind (not the body or world). The body is merely a physical instrument to facilitate our learning forgiveness in this incarnation.

ACIM References to BODY

Pg. 60T (Pg. 66T SE) - "The body is the ego's home by its own election. It is the only identification with which the ego feels safe, since the body's vulnerability is its own best argument that you cannot be of God."

Pg. 97T (Pg. 105T SE) - "The ego uses the body for attack, for pleasure and for pride. The insanity of this perception makes it a fearful one indeed. The Holy Spirit sees the body only as a means of communication, and because communicating is sharing it becomes communion."

Pg. 372T (Pg. 399T SE) - "The inevitable compromise is the belief that the body must be healed, and not the mind."

Pg. 412T (Pg. 442T SE) - "The body is the sign of weakness, vulnerability and loss of power. Can such a savior help you? Would you turn in your distress and need for help unto the helpless? Is the pitifully little the perfect choice to call upon for strength?"

7

BODY CONT'D

ACIM References to BODY Cont'd

Pg. 472T (Pg. 508T SE) - "Of itself the body can do nothing. See it as means to hurt, and it is hurt. See it as means to heal, and it is healed."

Pg. 30MT (Pg. 31MT SE) - "Yet what makes God's teachers is their recognition of the proper purpose of the body. As they advance in their profession, they become more and more certain that the body's function is but to let God's Voice speak through it to human ears."

CAUSE/EFFECT

CAUSE: Condition, Content, Means, Principle, Purpose

EFFECT: Act, Action, Behavior level, Consequence, Ends, Expressed, Expression, Form, Function, Method, Symptom

On Level One, God is the Cause, and His Son (Sonship) is the Effect. We, the Effect of God, are what makes God our Father (Cause). On either level, cause and effect are dependent on each other; the existence of one makes the other. You have to have an effect if there is a cause; therefore, you have to have a cause to have an effect.

An extremely important point that the *Course* points out is "ideas leave not their source," which means we can't be separate from God because Cause and Effect are one.

Our mind is the cause and our world (body) is the effect. That is why the *Course* says seek not to change the world, but our thinking about the world. Remember, "ideas leave not their source." What we project comes back. Also, what we extend comes back. Therefore, if our thoughts (cause) make our world, i.e., body (effect), it follows that when we change our thoughts (thinking), the purpose we give the world will reflect this change in our thinking. Keep in mind that our thinking never stops. Moreover, we only have two voices from which to choose (Holy Spirit or the ego).

ACIM References to CAUSE AND EFFECT

Pg. 28T (Pg. 32T SE) - "Actually, 'Cause' is a term properly belonging to God, and His 'Effect' is His Son."

Pg. 151T (Pg. 162T SE) - "Fear cannot be real without a cause, and God is the only Cause. God is Love and you do want Him. This *is* your will. Ask for this and you will be answered, because you will be asking only for what belongs to you."

9

CAUSE/EFFECT CONT'D

ACIM References to CAUSE AND EFFECT Cont'd

Pg. 480T (Pg. 516T SE) - "A co-creator with the Father must have a Son. Yet must this Son have been created like Himself. A perfect being, all-encompassing and all-encompassed, nothing to add and nothing taken from; not born of size nor place nor time, nor held to limits or uncertainties of any kind. Here do the means and end unite as one, nor does this one have any end at all."

Pg. 26WB (Pg. 26WB SE) - "The idea for today is a beginning step in dispelling the belief that your thoughts have no effect. Everything you see is the result of your thoughts. There is no exception to this fact. Thoughts are not big or little; powerful or weak. They are merely true or false. Those that are true create their own likeness. Those that are false make theirs. . . . Besides your recognizing that thoughts are never idle, salvation requires that you also recognize that every thought you have brings either peace or war; either love or fear. A neutral result is impossible because a neutral thought is impossible."

Pg. 28WB (Pg. 28WB SE) - "It is always the thought that comes first, despite the temptation to believe that it is the other way around."

CHRIST

Christ, when used by itself, does not refer to the embodiment of Jesus Christ. Christ is the essence or spiritual makeup within each of us.

It is the illusionary nature of the body and world that seem to separate us. The Christ nature that is in each of us makes up the body of Christ, which is the totality of the Sonship.

ACIM References to CHRIST

Pg. 473T (Pg. 509T SE) - "The Christ in you is very still. He looks on what He loves, and knows it is as Himself. And thus does He rejoice at what He sees, because He knows that it is one with Him and with His Father."

Pg. 421WB (Pg. 431WB SE) - "Christ is God's Son as He created Him. He is the Self we share, uniting us with one another, and with God as well. He is the Thought Which still abides within the Mind that is His Source. He has not left His holy home, nor lost the innocence in which He was created. He abides unchanged forever in the Mind of God. Christ is the link that keeps you one with God, and guarantees that separation is no more than an illusion of despair, for hope forever will abide in Him. Your mind is part of His, and His of yours. He is the part in which God's Answer lies; where all decisions are already made, and dreams are over. He remains untouched by anything the body's eyes perceive. For though in Him His Father placed the means for your salvation, yet does He remain the Self Who, like His Father, knows no sin."

CREATION AND CREATIONS

Creation refers to the extension of God. This extension would be His Son (Sonship), which includes everyone.

Creations refers to the love that is extended from one brother to another upon joining with the Holy Spirit.

ACIM References to CREATION and CREATIONS

Pg. 44T (Pg. 49T SE) - "Every system of thought must have a starting point. It begins with either a making or a creating, a difference we have already discussed. Their resemblance lies in their power as foundations. Their difference lies in what rests upon them. Both are cornerstones for systems of belief by which one lives."

Pg. 179T (Pg. 193T SE) - "You make by projection, but God creates by extension."

Pg. 451WB (Pg. 461WB SE) - "God's Thoughts are given all the power that their own Creator has. For He would add to Love by its extension. Thus His Son shares in creation, and must therefore share in power to create."

DEATH

The ego points to the fact we are a body, so upon death we cease to exist.

The Holy Spirit states that the body neither lives nor dies, is neither sick nor well, but is merely a learning device (vehicle) which we use to learn our lessons in forgiveness. Since we choose sickness, we also choose death. This choice can be made, as with everything else, with the ego or the Holy Spirit.

Upon death (laying down of the body), we are not united with our Creator. (We are already united.) The removal of guilt makes us aware of this unity, which is accomplished through forgiveness.

Note: The *Course* also refers to the ego as death, or our ego thoughts as death.

ACIM References to DEATH

Pg. 96T (Pg. 104T SE) - "When your body and your ego and your dreams are gone, you will know that you will last forever. Perhaps you think this is accomplished through death, but nothing is accomplished through death, because death is nothing. Everything is accomplished through life, and life is of the mind and in the mind. The body neither lives nor dies, because it cannot contain you who are life. If we share the same mind, you can overcome death because I did."

Pg. 388T (Pg. 416T SE) - "No one can die unless he chooses death. . . . When you accepted the Holy Spirit's purpose in place of the ego's you renounced death, exchanging it for life. We know that an idea leaves not its source. And death is the result of the thought we call the ego, as surely as life is the result of the Thought of God."

Pg. 389T (Pg. 417T SE) - "From the ego came sin and guilt and death, in opposition to life and innocence, and to the Will of God Himself."

13

DEATH CONT'D

ACIM References to DEATH Cont'd

Pg. 311WB (Pg. 318WB SE) - "You think that death is of the body. Yet it is but an idea, irrelevant to what is seen as physical. A thought is in the mind. It can be then applied as mind directs it. But its origin is where it must be changed, if change occurs. Ideas leave not their source. The emphasis this course has placed on that idea is due to its centrality in our attempts to change your mind about yourself. It is the reason you can heal. It is the cause of healing. It is why you cannot die. Its truth established you as one with God."

DEFENSES

Upon looking at our own guilt caused by the belief we separated from God, we find the fear inside of us unbearable. The ego rushes to our defense and assures us that it will get rid of our guilt for us. Accordingly, it then proceeds to project our guilt onto someone else. Upon witnessing this guilt in another, we become afraid and seek a defense from our own guilt. Remember, the guilt we "magically" gave to our brother only reinforces our own. The ego tells us another is the cause of our anger (bad guy), and we are the innocent victim (good guy). Therefore, the victimizer needs punishment; our defense (whether to attack now or later) is ready to protect us, since we feel God is incapable of coming to our defense.

From a Level One point of view, the world and body are defenses to keep God away. This was needed, since the belief in separation and usurping of God's power entered the split mind, making God vengeful.

ACIM References to DEFENSES

Pg. 16T (Pg. 19T SE) - "Everyone defends his treasure, and will do so automatically. The real questions are, what do you treasure? and how much do you treasure it?"

Pg. 33WB (Pg. 33WB SE) - "Today's idea accurately describes the way anyone who holds attack thoughts in his mind must see the world. Having projected his anger onto the world, he sees vengeance about to strike at him. His own attack is thus perceived as self defense."

Pg. 245WB (Pg. 252WB SE) - "Defense is frightening. It stems from fear, increasing fear as each defense is made. You think it offers safety. Yet it speaks of fear made real and terror justified. Is it not strange you do not pause to ask, as you elaborate your plans and make your armor thicker and your locks more tight, what you defend, and how, and against what? Let us consider first what you defend. It must be something that is very weak and easily assaulted. It must be something made easy prey, unable to protect itself and needing your defense. What but the body has such frailty that constant care and watchful, deep concern are needful to protect its little life? What but the body falters and must fail to serve the Son of God as worthy host?"

15

DENIAL

In the ego's arsenal, there are two defense mechanisms, and the first one used is denial. As the *Course* and psychotherapists will tell you, the worst thing to do in a situation is to deny it happened.

This is what the ego wants you to do because when you deny, the ego says you no longer have the problem. When you do this you are denying the Holy Spirit's help. How can He help you if you say you don't have a problem? The Holy Spirit's use of denial is to deny error (mistake) and to affirm Truth (God, Holy Spirit, Jesus). What this means is you deny the use the ego has employed (separation, guilt and attack) and substitute joining, forgiveness and love.

On a Level One point of view, we deny we separated from God. The *Course* refers to this as "the veil of forgetfulness" or the "veil of denial." Veils are used throughout the *Course* and refer to denial.

From a Level Two point of view, after projecting our guilt onto someone or something, we magically forget or deny it.

ACIM References to DENIAL

Pg. 16T (Pg. 19T SE) - "True denial is a powerful protective device. You can and should deny any belief that error can hurt you. This kind of denial is not a concealment but a correction."

Pg. 203T (Pg. 218T SE) - "Miracles are merely the translation of denial into truth."

DEVIL

In the *Course's* view, the word *devil* is just another name for the ego. It is seldom used in any of the three (3) books comprising the *Course*. It is actually what the ego projects (sin and guilt) onto something external.

ACIM References to DEVIL

Pg. 44T (Pg. 49T SE) - "The 'devil' is a frightening concept because he seems to be extremely powerful and extremely active. He is perceived as a force in combat with God, battling Him for possession of His creations. The devil deceives by lies, and builds kingdoms in which everything is in direct opposition to God. Yet he attracts men rather than repels them, and they are willing to 'sell' him their souls in return for gifts of no real worth. This makes absolutely no sense."

Pg. 45T (Pg. 50T SE) - "The mind can make the belief in separation very real and very fearful, and this belief *is* the 'devil.' It is powerful, active, destructive and clearly in opposition to God, because it literally denies His Fatherhood."

EGO: Anti-Christ, Grandiosity, Littleness,
Self Concept, Untrue, Untruth

The ego is the belief in the reality of separation. From this point of view, our belief shows us that we can be separated both from God and our brother. At the moment the thought of separation entered our mind, we created a false self to substitute for our true Self. This thought of separation gave rise to guilt, fear, the manifestation of the body and the belief in attack to defend oneself.

The ego is the part of the split mind that believes it is separated from the Mind of Christ. It can be looked upon as the analytical mind.

ACIM References to EGO

Pg. 37T (Pg. 42T SE) -"The ego is the wrong-minded attempt to perceive yourself as you wish to be, rather than as you are."

Pg. 55T (Pg. 60T SE) - "It is surely apparent by now why the ego regards Spirit as its 'enemy.' The ego arose from the separation, and its continued existence depends on your continuing belief in the separation. The ego must offer you some sort of reward for maintaining this belief. All it can offer is a sense of temporary existence, which begins with its own beginning and ends with its own ending. It tells you this life is your existence because it is its own."

Pg. 61T (Pg. 67T SE) - "The ego does not recognize the real source of 'threat', and if you associate yourself with the ego, you do not understand the situation as it is. Only your allegiance to it gives the ego any power over you."

Pg. 164T (Pg. 175T SE) - "The ego is also in your mind, because you have accepted it there. Its evaluation of you, however, is the exact opposite of the Holy Spirit's, because the ego does not love you."

Pg. 207T (Pg. 223T SE) - "The ego is certain that love is dangerous, and this is always its central teaching. It never puts it this way; on the contrary, everyone who believes that the ego is salvation seems to be intensely engaged in the search for love."

18

EXTENSION: Christ Vision, Create, Vision

The extension principle works and has the same properties as those of projection, except that the starting point is different. As in the ego's projection principle, the starting point is guilt, and this is what you project.

In extension, the starting point is love (Holy Spirit), and the word the *Course* uses now is "extension." In this process you are not trying to get rid of something (separation), but attempting to join with what you see.

In both extension and projection, whatever you give away will come back. A Level One example of extension would be the process by which God extends Himself. This process created the Sonship. A Level Two example of extension would be that when we join with the Holy Spirit, our love automatically extends to our brother without any action on our part.

ACIM References to EXTENSION

Pg. 91T (Pg. 98T SE) - "The ego projects to exclude, and therefore to deceive. The Holy Spirit extends by recognizing Himself in every mind, and thus perceives them as one."

Pg. 179T (Pg. 193T SE) - "You make by projection, but God creates by extension."

Pg. 449T (Pg. 482T SE) - "Extension of forgiveness is the Holy Spirit's function. Leave this to Him. Let your concern be only that you give to Him that which can be extended."

19

FACE OF CHRIST: Face of Innocence

When using these words (Face of Christ), the *Course* does not mean we will literally see the Face of Christ. It is referring to purity, love, and the oneness with our brother. It can be called the Face of Innocence, whereby we join with our brother, through Christ. (See Forgiveness) As in everything to which this *Course* refers, the Face of Christ, or the Face of Innocence, has nothing to do with physical sight.

ACIM References to FACE OF CHRIST

Pg. 403T (Pg. 433T SE) - "To each who walks this earth in seeming solitude is a savior given, whose special function here is to release him, and so to free himself. In the world of separation each is appointed separately, though they are all the same. Yet those who know that they are all the same need not salvation. And each one finds his savior when he is ready to look upon the face of Christ, and see Him sinless."

Pg. 65MT (Pg. 68MT SE) - "The resurrection is the denial of death, being the assertion of life. Thus is all the thinking of the world reversed entirely. Life is now recognized as salvation, and pain and misery of any kind perceived as hell. Love is no longer feared, but gladly welcomed. Idols have disappeared, and the rememberance of God shines unimpeded across the world. Christ's face is seen in every living thing, and nothing is held in darkness, apart from the light of forgiveness."

Pg. 79MT (Pg. 83MT SE) - "*The face of Christ* has to be seen before the memory of God can return. The reason is obvious. Seeing the face of Christ involves perception. No one can look on knowledge. But the face of Christ is the great symbol of forgiveness. It is salvation. It is the symbol of the real world. Whoever looks on this no longer sees the world. He is near as to Heaven as is possible outside the gate. Yet from this gate it is no more than just a step inside. It is the final step. And this we leave to God."

20

FORGIVENESS: Atonement, Bridge, Correct perception, Joining, Right perception, True perception, Salvation

First, let's explain what forgiveness is not. Forgiveness, from the ego's point of view, would be to first look at the error the person has committed and then, because we are better than he, we forgive him. We can see how the ego keeps us away from truth once more. First, he makes the error real, which means we blame someone in the world (effect) for our problems. Now he tells us we are better (unequal), and now we try to forgive. This is not forgiveness; it is impossible, **and I mean impossible**, to forgive someone we feel has hurt us.

Now let's look at the three steps the Holy Spirit utilizes in forgiveness. First (and from my point of view), the hardest for most people to grasp is the concept that *we* are the cause of our problems (see cause and effect). The second step entails looking at our problems without judgment and having a little willingness to turn them over to the Holy Spirit. Notice it doesn't say a lot of willingness, because if we had a lot of willingness, we wouldn't need this *Course* or have the need to forgive in the first place. Upon completing steps one and two, our part is finished. The third step is the Holy Spirit's, for He removes the guilt from within (cause).

ACIM References to FORGIVENESS

Pg. 41T (Pg. 46T SE) - "Forgiveness is the healing of the perception of separation. Correct perception of your brother is necessary, because minds have chosen to see themselves as separate."

Pg. 54T (Pg. 59T SE) - "The whole value of right perception lies in the inevitable realization that all perception is unnecessary. This removes the block entirely."

Pg. 510T (Pg. 548T SE) - "And what has been forgiven must join, for nothing stands between to keep them separate and apart."

Pg. 34WB (Pg. 34WB SE) - "You see the world that you have made, but you do not see yourself as the image-maker. You cannot be saved from the world, but you can escape from its cause. This is what salvation means, for where is

21

FORGIVENESS CONT'D

ACIM References to FORGIVENESS Cont'd

Pg. 34WB (Pg. 34WB SE) Cont'd - the world you see when its cause is gone? Vision already holds a replacement for everything you think you see now. Loveliness can light your images, and so transform them that you will love them, even though they were made of hate.

Pg. 34WB (Pg. 34WB SE) Cont'd - For you will not be making them alone. . . . . The idea for today introduces the thought that you are not trapped in the world you see, because its cause can be changed. This change requires, first, that the cause be identified and then let go, so that it can be replaced. The first two steps in this process require your cooperation. The final one does not. Your images have already been replaced. By taking the first two steps, you will see that this is so."

Pg. 391WB (Pg. 401WB SE) - "Forgiveness recognizes what you thought your brother did to you has not occurred. It does not pardon sins and make them real. It sees there was no sin. And in that view are all your sins forgiven. What is sin, except a false idea about God's Son? Forgiveness merely sees its falsity, and therefore lets it go. What then is free to take its place is now the Will of God."

FORM: Effect

The word *form* is always associated with the body and world. It is at this level that the ego says our problems exist. So it is there that the ego says we solve them. (See Cause and Effect.)

ACIM Reference to FORM

Pg. 442T (Pg. 475T SE) - "Only the form of error attracts the ego. Meaning it does not recognize, and does not see if it is there or not. Everything the body's eyes see is a mistake, an error in perception, a distorted fragment of the whole without the meaning that the whole would give. And yet mistakes, regardless of their form, can be corrected."

FUNCTION

The word *function* is written on two levels. A reference to the function of God means that God's function is extending Himself, thereby creating the Sonship. This process is a Level One experience.

In the world, we all have the same function (forgiveness), though we will meet different people in our lives. Therefore, on the form level, the lessons will appear different. This would be a reference to *function* on a Level Two basis.

ACIM References to FUNCTION

Pg. 123T (Pg. 132T SE) - "The extension of God's Being is spirit's only function."

Pg. 260T (Pg. 280T SE) - "Your function here is only to decide against deciding what you want, in recognition that you do not know. How, then, can you decide what you should do? Leave all decisions to the One Who speaks for God, and for your function as He knows it."

Pg. 403T (Pg. 433T SE) - "To each who walks this earth in seeming solitude is a savior given, whose special function here is to release him, and so to free himself."

Pg 493T (Pg. 530T SE) - "The Holy Spirit needs your special function, that His may be fulfilled."

Pg. 53MT (Pg. 55MT SE) - "The teacher of God has taken accepting the Atonement for himself as his only function."

GAP: Separation, Space

A gap is anything that we put between us and our brother, or between God and ourselves. The following things cause gaps (separation) between us: sickness, hate, anger, the world and the body.

ACIM References to GAP

Pg. 558T (Pg. 601T SE) - "What is there God created to be sick? And what that He created not can be? Let not your eyes behold a dream; your ears bear witness to illusion. They were made to look upon a world that is not there; to hear the voices that can make no sound. Yet are there other sounds and other sights that *can* be seen and heard and understood. For eyes and ears are senses without sense, and what they see and hear they but report. It is not they that hear and see, but you, who put together every jagged piece, each senseless scrap and shred of evidence, and make a witness to the world you want. Let not the body's ears and eyes perceive these countless fragments seen within the gap that you imagined, and let them persuade their maker his imaginings are real."

Pg. 559T (Pg. 602T SE) - "Creation proves reality because it shares the function all creation shares. It is not made of little bits of glass, a piece of wood, a thread or two, perhaps, all put together to attest its truth. Reality does not depend on this. There is no gap that separates the truth from dreams and from illusions."

Pg. 560T (Pg. 603T SE) - "The body represents the gap between the little bit of mind you call your own and all the rest of what is really yours."

Pg. 561T (Pg. 604T SE) - "A space where God is not, a gap between the Father and the Son is not the Will of either, who have promised to be one. God's promise is a promise to Himself, and there is no one who could be untrue to what He wills as part of what He is. The promise that there is no gap between Himself and what He is cannot be false. What will can come between what must be one, and in Whose Wholeness there can be no gap?"

25

GAP CONT'D

ACIM References to GAP Cont'd

Pg. 568T (Pg. 611T SE) - "You cannot wake yourself. Yet you can let yourself be wakened. You can overlook your brother's dreams. So perfectly can you forgive him his illusions he becomes your savior from your dreams. And as you see him shining in the space of light where God abides within the darkness, you will see that God Himself is where his body is."

GIFT

God's gift is love, which is always with us although we can deny it. God's gifts are given to us by the Holy Spirit through forgiveness. Through our joining with the Holy Spirit, on the form level, it seems as though God gives us things. Actually, what happens is that we remove the obstacles (sin, guilt, fear, etc.) from our minds, and this opens up our awareness to our loving thoughts. Peace, love, and joy can now come into our lives. These gifts are actually the effect of our oneness with God.

The ego's gifts are: guilt, sickness, death, fear, and separation; they are acquired through specialness.

ACIM References to GIFT

Pg. 120T (Pg. 129T SE) - "The gifts you offer to the ego are always experienced as sacrifices, but the gifts you offer to the Kingdom are gifts to you. They will always be treasured by God because they belong to His Beloved Sons, who belong to Him. All power and glory are yours because the Kingdom is His."

Pg. 543T (Pg. 585T SE) - "Brother, He gives but life. Yet what you see as gifts your brother offers represent the gifts you dream your Father gives to you. Let all your brother's gifts be seen in light of charity and kindness offered you. And let no pain disturb your dream of deep appreciation for his gifts to you."

Pg. 183WB (Pg. 186WB SE) - "Today's idea continues with the thought that joy and peace are not but idle dreams. They are your right, because of what you are. They come to you from God, Who cannot fail to give you what He wills. Yet must there be a place made ready to receive His gifts. They are not welcomed gladly by a mind that has instead received the gifts it made where His belong as substitutes for them."

Pg. 367WB (Pg. 377WB SE) - "It does not matter if another thinks your gifts unworthy. In his mind there is a part that joins with yours in thanking you. It does not matter if your gifts seem lost and ineffectual. They are received

GIFT CONT'D

ACIM References to GIFT

Pg. 367WB (Pg. 377WB SE) Cont'd - where they are given. In your gratitude are they accepted universally, and thankfully acknowledged by the Heart of God Himself. And would you take them back, when He has gratefully accepted them? God blesses every gift you give to Him, and every gift is given Him, because it can be given only to yourself."

GOD: All, Cause, Creator, Father,
Holy One, Knowledge, Love,
Magnitude, Perfect Creator,
Truth, Unalterable, Beginning

The Course's definition of God is one of omnipresence, all encompassing and our Creator. Given this definition, we are one with Him and have only His attributes. Being all encompassing, He can have no opposite; therefore, anything not of God is an illusion.

The ego's view of God is a god of fear. Since we all have bought into the ego's thought system, we believe we have separated from God and in so doing we feel we have usurped His power. Therefore, we feel guilty at the deepest core of our being. Feeling guilty, we must project it and, on a Level One, we project our guilt onto God. Now God changes from a God of love to a god of fear. This god now demands punishment for our sins. Remember, guilt always demands punishment.

ACIM References to GOD

Pg. 299T (Pg. 321T SE) - "God does not understand your problem in communication for He does not share it with you."

Pg. 492T (Pg. 529T SE) - "He can see no evil; nothing in the world to fear, and no one who is different from himself. And as he loves them, so he looks upon himself with love and gentleness. He would no more condemn himself for his mistakes than damn another. He is not an arbiter of vengeance, nor a punisher of sin. The kindness of his sight rests on himself with all the tenderness it offers others. For he would only heal and only bless. And being in accord with what God wills, he has the power to heal and bless all those he looks on with the grace of God upon his sight."

Pg. 73WB (Pg. 75WB SE) - "God does not forgive because He has never condemned. And there must be condemnation before forgiveness is necessary."

29

GREAT RAYS

The Great Rays are merely the reflection (*effect of God's Love or Light.*) They are of truth and spirit, therefore, have nothing to do with the ego.

In our perceptual world, the Great Rays represent the light of Christ which is in each of us. This is made visible through forgiveness (Vision).

ACIM References to Great Rays

Pg. 175T (Pg. 189T SE) - "The power of one mind can shine into another, because all the lamps of God were lit by the same spark. It is everywhere and it is eternal. In many only the spark remains, for the Great Rays are obscured. Yet God has kept the spark alive so that the Rays can never be completely forgotten. If you but see the little spark you will learn of the greater light, for the Rays are there unseen. Perceiving the spark will heal, but knowing the light will create. Yet in the returning the little light must be acknowledged first, for the separation was a descent from magnitude to littleness. But the spark is still as pure as the great light, because it is the remaining call of creation. Put all your faith in it, and God Himself will answer you."

Pg. 299T (Pg. 322T SE) - "As the ego would limit your perception of your brothers to the body, so would the Holy Spirit release your vision and let you see the Great Rays shining from them, so unlimited that they reach to God."

GUILT: Cloud bank, Dark clouds

Ultimately, on Level One, all guilt feelings (feelings of inadequacy, anger, fear, never being good enough, feelings of the need to be punished, etc.) come from the belief that we have separated from God. In reality, this never happened, therefore, we have nothing to forgive or feel guilty about. Given the fact that we do believe we have separated from God and usurped His power, we feel guilty at the core of our being (most guilt is experienced *subconsciously* and we feel that God will punish us). After having done a sinful act, we must feel guilty, and since guilt always demands punishment, on this level we feel God is the one who will punish us.

On Level Two, guilt is experienced between our brothers and sisters. This act of separation (attack) makes us feel incomplete, guilty and not whole, and since feeling guilty is the last thing we want to experience, we seek its removal. In the ego's arsenal, this is accomplished through projection and then denial.

ACIM References to GUILT

Pg. 77T (Pg. 83T SE) - "Guilt is more than merely not of God. It is the symbol of attack on God."

Pg 223T (Pg. 239T SE) - "The ultimate purpose of projection is always to get rid of guilt. . . . You cannot dispel guilt by making it real, and then atoning for it. This is the ego's plan, which it offers instead of dispelling it. . . . . Yet consider how strange a solution the ego's arrangement is. You project guilt to get rid of it, but you are actually merely concealing it. You do experience the guilt, but you have no idea why."

Pg. 43MT (Pg. 45MT SE) - "And herein lies the birthplace of guilt. Who usurps the place of God and takes it for himself now has a deadly 'enemy' and he must stand alone in his protection, and make himself a shield to keep him safe from fury that can never be abated, and vengeance that can never be satisfied."

31

HEALING: Joining

Healing *(joining)* is the undoing of sickness *(separation)*. It has nothing to do with the body, because the body is never sick. It is the mind that is sick, and this sick mind projects our guilt onto our body.

Healing is accomplished by joining our mind with the Holy Spirit *(right-mindedness)*. This process makes us whole.

Any attempt to heal at the form level reinforces our belief in magic. As sickness is in the mind, healing must also take place there.

ACIM References to HEALING

Pg. 105T (Pg. 114T SE) - "To heal is the only kind of thinking in this world that resembles the Thought of God, and because of the elements they share, can transfer easily to it."

Pg. 373T (Pg. 400T SE) - "You see the Christ in him, and he is healed because you look on what makes faith forever justified in every one."

Pg. 21MT (Pg. 22MT SE) - "For a teacher of God to remain concerned about the result of healing is to limit the healing. It is now the teacher of God himself whose mind needs to be healed. . . . Whenever a teacher of God has tried to be a channel for healing he has succeeded. . . . One of the most difficult temptations to recognize is that to doubt a healing because of the appearance of continuing symptoms is a mistake in the form of lack of trust."

Pg. 53MT (Pg. 55MT SE) - "Healing and Atonement are not related; they are identical. There is no order of difficulty in miracles because there are no degrees of Atonement. . . . To forgive is to heal. . . . That forgiveness is healing needs to be understood, if the teacher of God is to make progress."

HEAVEN: Kingdom

Heaven is the state where God and His creations come together. It is a place where only the world of God and His Sonship exists. The closest thing to Heaven that we are able to understand, given our limited perception, would be the Holy Instant.

ACIM References to HEAVEN

Pg. 77T (Pg. 83T SE) - "In Heaven there is no guilt, because the Kingdom is attained through the Atonement, which releases you to create."

Pg. 282T (Pg. 303T SE) - "Time is inconceivable without change, yet holiness does not change. Learn from this instant more than merely that hell does not exist. In this redeeming instant lies Heaven. And Heaven will not change, for the birth into the holy present is salvation from change."

Pg. 509T (Pg. 548T SE) - "Forgiveness is this world's equivalent of Heaven's justice. It translates the world of sin into a simple world, where justice can be reflected from beyond the gate behind which total lack of limits lies."

HELL

In one aspect, hell has the same meaning as the hell of traditional Christianity, a world after death where we are punished for our sins. It also means the belief that we must suffer in the future for our past mistakes. Both of the above meanings are ego based. In the spirit realm (God) hell is impossible because God has no opposite, and we never separated from Him. God is all inclusive and omnipresent.

All ego thoughts can also be thought of as hell.

ACIM References to HELL

Pg. 280T (Pg. 301T SE) - "The ego is an ally of time, but not a friend. For it is as misrustful of death as it is of life, and what it wants for you it cannot tolerate. The ego wants *you* dead, but not itself. The outcome of its strange religion must therefore be the conviction that it can pursue you beyond the grave. And out of its unwillingness for you to find peace even in death, it offers you immortality in hell. It speaks to you of Heaven, but assures you that Heaven is not for you. How can the guilty hope for Heaven? The belief in hell is inescapable to those who identify with the ego."

Pg. 281T (Pg. 302T SE) - "The Holy Spirit teaches thus: There is no hell. Hell is only what the ego has made of the present."

Pg. 232WB (Pg. 238WB SE) - "Accept a little part of hell as real, and you have damned your eyes and cursed your sight, and what you will behold is hell indeed."

Pg. 257WB (Pg. 264WB SE) - "In this world Heaven is a choice, because here we believe there are alternatives to choose between. We think that all things have an opposite, and what we want we choose. If Heaven exists there must be hell as well, for contradiction is the way we make what we perceive, and what we think is real. . . . Creation knows no opposite."

Pg. 36MT (Pg. 37MT SE) - "To turn hell into Heaven is the function of God's teachers, for what they teach are lessons in which Heaven is reflected."

ACIM References to HELL Cont'd

Pg. 83MT (Pg. 88MT SE) - "He will remain with you to lead you from the hell you made to God."

HOLY INSTANT

This is another phrase that is greatly misunderstood. It is simply the instant, or interval of time, that we choose to listen to the Holy Spirit's voice instead of the ego's voice.

In the holy instant, we are living in the "now", which at one level is the closest thing to the eternal. By choosing the ego we constantly live in the past. This keeps us in "hell" and keeps us from experiencing God.

We experience the holy instant numerous times throughout the day. This is usually experienced in short intervals. The *Course*, through forgiveness, allows us to experience the holy instant for longer and longer periods of time. Eventually this is all we will experience, which means we are in constant communication with God and living in the real world.

ACIM References to HOLY INSTANT

Pg. 284T (Pg. 306T SE) - "Start now to practice your little part in separating out the holy instant. You will receive very specific instructions as you go along. To learn to separate out this single second, and to experience it as timeless, is to begin to experience yourself as not separate. Fear not that you will not be given help in this. God's Teacher and His lesson will support your strength."

Pg. 534T (Pg. 576T SE) - "The holy instant is the interval in which the mind is still enough to hear an answer that is not entailed within the question asked. It offers something new and different from the question. How could it be answered if it but repeats itself?"

HOLY RELATIONSHIP

First, let me explain an unholy relationship. This type of relationship starts out with the ego saying we are lacking, not complete. Feeling the need for completion, and listening to the ego's voice, we are directed to the world for completion. The ego says this person will make us complete. Actually what we have is a dependent relationship where the other person supplies our need. You see how nicely in this type of relationship the ego keeps us away from God.

A holy relationship starts with the same premise, that we are lacking, but the Holy Spirit tells us what will make us complete is God. Upon forming relationships now, they come not out of dependency but as a need to extend our Love.

Very seldom does the *Course* refer to relationships with things (food, drugs, etc.) in the world.

ACIM References to HOLY RELATIONSHIP

Pg. 404T (Pg. 434T SE) - "In this world, God's Son comes closest to himself in a holy relationship."

Pg. 407T (Pg. 437T SE) - "The Holy Spirit's temple is not a body, but a relationship."

Pg. 435T (Pg. 467T SE) - "For an unholy relationship is based on differences, where each one thinks the other has what he has not. They come together, each to complete himself and rob the other. They stay until they think that there is nothing left to steal, and then move on. . . . A holy relationship starts from a different premise. Each one has looked within and seen no lack. Accepting his completion, he would extend it by joining with another, whole as himself. He sees no difference between these selves, for differences are only of the body. Therefore, he looks on nothing he would take. He denies not his own reality *because* it is the truth. Just under Heaven does he stand, but close enough not to return to earth. For this relationship has Heaven's holiness.

37

ACIM References to HOLY RELATIONSHIP Cont'd

Pg. 435T (Pg. 467T SE) Cont'd - How far from home can a relationship so like to Heaven be? Think what a holy relationship can teach! Here is belief in differences undone. Here is the faith in difference shifted to sameness. And reason now can lead you and your brother to the logical conclusion of your union. It must extend, as you extended when you joined."

HOLY SPIRIT: Answer, Comforter, Communication Link, Correction, Eternal Guest, Eternal Guide, Friend, God's Answer, God's Teacher, Great Transformer, Mediator, Redeemer, Right-mindedness, Teacher, Teacher of Reality, Therapist, Translator, Universal Giver, Universal Inspiration, Voice for God, Voice for Love, Voice for Peace

The Holy Spirit is God's Answer to the separation. He is the communications link between God and His separated sons. The Holy Spirit can be seen as a middle man between God and ourselves. He serves as a bridge to God, for without Him, the distance would be too great.

He can see our mistakes (illusions) but leads us past them to Truth. This is done through forgiveness (true perception). This is accomplished in our perceptual world where we have choices. He represents the other choice, which is always to join, so both can gain. He represents God and, therefore, shows us the Love in everyone. We can't see Him, but we can see his manifestations.

ACIM References to HOLY SPIRIT

Pg. 70T (Pg. 76T SE) - "The Holy Spirit is your Guide in choosing. He is in the part of your mind that always speaks for the right choice, because He speaks for God. He is your remaining communication with God, which you can interrupt but cannot destroy. The Holy Spirit is the way in which God's Will is done on earth as it is in Heaven."

Pg. 73T (Pg. 79T SE) - "The Holy Spirit is the mediator between the interpretations of the ego and the knowledge of the spirit. His ability to deal with symbols enables Him to work with the ego's beliefs in its own language. His ability to look beyond symbols into eternity enables Him to understand the laws of God, for which He speaks. He can therefore perform the function of reinterpreting what the ego makes, not by destruction but by understanding. Understanding is light, but you yourself do not know this. It is therefore the task of the Holy Spirit to reinterpret you on behalf of God."

39

ACIM References to HOLY SPIRIT Cont'd

Pg. 161T (Pg. 172T SE) - "The Holy Spirit is the only Therapist. He makes healing clear in any situation in which He is the Guide. You can only let Him fulfill His function. He needs no help for this. He will tell you exactly what to do to help anyone He sends to you for help, and will speak to him through you if you do not interfere."

Pg. 214T (Pg. 230T SE) - "The Holy Spirit is invisible, but you can see the results of His Presence, and through them you will learn that He is there. What He enables you to do is clearly not of this world, for miracles violate every law of reality as this world judges it. Every law of time and space, of magnitude and mass is transcended, for what the Holy Spirit enables you to do is clearly beyond all of them. Perceiving His results, you will understand where He must be, and finally know what He is."

IDOLS: Anti Christ

Idols are substitutes or replacements for the love we feel God cannot, or will not give us. That makes the world and the body our idols.

Therefore, what we worship (feel will being us joy) becomes an idol to take the place of God. Similarly, what brings us pain (sickness, unholy relationships) also becomes idols, because we worship them instead of God. In this case, idols can also be looked upon as defenses which keep us from the love of God.

ACIM References to IDOLS

Pg. 409T (Pg. 438T SE) - "The body is the ego's idol; the belief in sin made flesh and then projected outward."

Pg. 576T (Pg. 620T SE) - "This world of idols is a veil across the face of Christ, because its purpose is to separate your brother from yourself."

Pg. 586T (Pg. 631T SE) - "Behind the search for every idol lies the yearning for completion. Wholeness has no form because it is unlimited. To seek a special person or a thing to add to you to make yourself complete, can only mean that you believe some form is missing. And by finding this, you will achieve completion in a form you like. This is the purpose of an idol; that you will not look beyond it, to the source of the belief that you are incomplete. Only if you had sinned could this be so. For sin is the idea you are alone and separated off from what is whole. And thus it would be necessary for the search for wholeness to be made beyond the boundaries of limits on yourself."

ILLUSIONS: Fantasy, Unreal, False

The *Course* points out that we believe many things are real, but in reality they are not. Anything that is not of God is an illusion. A Level One example of illusions is the belief that we have separated from God. A Level Two example of illusions takes place after the thought of separation. This thought gave rise to the ego, where the world of bodies was projected outward. The body and the world would, therefore, have to be of an illusionary nature. What we must keep in mind is that we believe the separation occurred, therefore, we believe we are a body and live in a physical world. This is where the Holy Spirit reaches us. He shows us that what we made out of guilt can be given a new meaning. Where there were thoughts of separation, anger, and attack, now can be seen as thoughts of love, joining, and a genuine compassion for our brother. All this is accomplished through the act of forgiveness.

It could be helpful to substitute the word *neutral* for *illusionary* on Level Two. This should only be used as an aid, for eventually, in the Holy Instant, you will realize that the world and body are illusionary.

ACIM References to ILLUSIONS

Pg. 103T (Pg. 111T SE) - "Truth is without illusions and therefore within the Kingdom. Everything outside the Kingdom is illusion. When you threw truth away you saw yourself as if you were without it."

Pg. 188T (Pg. 202T SE) - "No one can escape from illusions unless he looks at them, for not looking is the way they are protected. There is no need to shrink from illusions, for they cannot be dangerous. We are ready to look more closely at the ego's thought system because together we have the lamp that will dispel it, and since you realize you do not want it, you must be ready. The "dynamics" of the ego will be our lesson for a while, for we must look first at this to see beyond it, since you have made it real. We will undo this error together, and then look beyond it to the truth. What is healing but the removal of all that stands in the way of knowledge? And how else can one dispel illusions except by looking at them directly, without protecting them?"

ILLUSIONS CONT'D

ACIM References to ILLUSIONS Cont'd

Pg. 325T (Pg. 350T SE) - "Remember that you always choose between truth and illusion; between the real Atonement that would heal and the ego's "atonement" that would destroy."

JESUS: Prince of Peace, Friend, Redeemer, Ancient Friend

Jesus is the *person* (I use this term for lack of a better word) who dictated the *Course* to Helen Schucman. Whenever the word *"I"* appears in the *Course*, it is referring to Jesus. Throughout the book, Jesus wants us to look to Him as a Friend, or elder brother, who is in charge of the atonement plan.

When trouble seems to threaten us, the *Course* wants us to pray to either God, Jesus or the Holy Spirit. In this sense, it makes no difference to whom you pray, inasmuch as they are not in competition. Technically, their function is different, but their goal is the same (removing guilt and getting us *back home*).

The word *"Jesus"* is not used exclusively with the word *"Christ"*, because Christ is in each of us. It refers to Jesus as the manifestation of the Holy Spirit. What that means is, since the Holy Spirit is egoless, Jesus has to be egoless.

On Level One, we are equal with Jesus because the separation never happened, but in time we are different. As the *Course* states, "We are guilty in time but guiltless in Eternity."

ACIM References to JESUS

Pg. 5T (Pg. 8T SE) - "I am higher because without me the distance between God and man would be too great for you to encompass. I bridge the distance as an elder brother to you on the one hand, and as a Son of God on the other. My devotion to my brothers has placed me in charge of the Sonship, which I render complete because I share it."

Pg. 6T (Pg. 8T SE) - "I am in charge of the process of Atonement, which I undertook to begin. When you offer a miracle to any of my brothers, you do it to *yourself* and me. The reason you come before me is that I do not need

44

ACIM References to JESUS Cont'd

Pg. 6T (Pg. 8T SE) Cont'd - miracles for my own Atonement, but I stand at the end in case you fail temporarily. My part in the Atonement is the cancelling out of all errors that you could not otherwise correct."

Pg. 50T (Pg. 56T SE) - "I will substitute for your ego if you wish, but never for your spirit. A father can safely leave a child with an elder brother who has shown himself responsible, but this involves no confusion about the child's origin."

JUDGMENT

Judgment is probably one of the most misunderstood words in the *Course*. In the *ego's* view, judgment implies condemnation. This means we choose who is "good" and who is "bad", and our opinion, or judgment, depends upon their actions (form). Therefore, if a brother changes his "bad" actions (form) he becomes the "good" guy.

The reason why we can't judge is that we judge the effect, not the cause. As in the principle of forgiveness, we are not the ones who forgive; therefore, we are not the ones who can judge. It is the Holy Spirit who does the judging. And His judgment is always, God's Son is guiltless.

All we need to do is let the Holy Spirit judge through us, and for us. Keep in mind, there are only two voices to whom you listen. If we don't let the Holy Spirit judge for us, we are letting the ego judge for us. There are no other alternatives.

ACIM References to JUDGMENT

Pg. 102T (Pg. 110T SE) - "Choosing through the Holy Spirit will lead you to the Kingdom."

Pg. 290T (Pg. 312T SE) - "The holy instant is the Holy Spirit's most useful learning device for teaching you love's meaning. For its purpose is to suspend judgment entirely. Judgment always rests on the past, for past experience is the basis on which you judge. Judgment becomes impossible without the past, for without it you do not understand anything. You would make no attempt to judge, because it would be quite apparent to you that you do not understand what anything means. You are afraid of this because you believe that without the ego, all would be chaos. Yet I assure you that without the ego, all would be love."

Pg. 545T (Pg. 587T SE) - "In gentle laughter does the Holy Spirit perceive the cause, and looks not to effects. How else would He correct your error,

46

JUDGMENT CONT'D

ACIM References to JUDGMENT Cont'd

Pg. 545T (Pg. 587T SE) cont'd - who have overlooked the cause entirely? He bids you bring each terrible effect to Him that you may look together on its foolish cause and laugh with Him a while. *You* judge effects, but *He* has judged their cause."

Pg. 26MT (Pg. 27MT SE) - "Judgment, like other devices by which the world of illusions is maintained, is totally misunderstood by the world. It is actually confused with wisdom, and substitutes for truth. As the world uses the term, an individual is capable of "good" and "bad" judgment, and his education aims at strengthening the former and minimizing the latter. . . . It is necessary for the teacher of God to realize, not that he should not judge, but that he cannot. In giving up judgment, he is merely giving up what he did not have. He gives up an illusion; or better, he has an illusion of giving up. He has actually merely become more honest. Recognizing that judgment was always impossible for him, he no longer attempts it. This is no sacrifice. On the contrary, he puts himself in a position where judgment *through* him rather than *by* him can occur. And this judgment is neither "good" nor "bad"."

JUSTICE

Justice, from the *ego's* point of view, means if you sin, you will pay for your mistake by being punished. In this way you balance out your wrong.

The Holy Spirit's use of justice means merely correcting your view *(perception)*. This means that upon seeing a presumed injustice which upsets you, you must realize the cause of the problem is in you, not in the other person, which means the only reason this person came into your life was to show you that you need help. His cry for help is your cry for help. If you deny the help that he needs, you deny the Holy Spirit helping you.

ACIM References to JUSTICE

Pg. 497T (Pg. 535T SE) - "There is a kind of justice in salvation of which the world knows nothing. To the world, justice and vengeance are the same, for sinners see justice only as their punishment, perhaps sustained by someone else, but not escaped. The laws of sin demand a victim. Who it may be makes little difference. But death must be the cost and must be paid. This is not justice, but insanity."

Page 502T (Pg. 540T SE) - "No one can be unjust to you, unless you have decided first to *be* unjust."

Pg. 507T (Pg. 545T SE) - "There is no such thing as partial justice. If the Son of God is guilty then is he condemned, and he deserves no mercy from the God of justice. . . . Forgiveness is the world's equivalent of Heaven's justice. It translates the world of sin into a simple world, where justice can be reflected from beyond the gate behind which total lack of limits lies."

<u>LAST STEP</u>: Final Step

This step is undertaken by God. It occurs when complete forgiveness *(Atonement)* has been accomplished. This process removes all ego thoughts and unites us with our Creator, whereupon God reaches down, grasps our hand, and takes us back unto Himself.

On Level One, this can't happen, strictly speaking, because the separation never occurred.

<u>ACIM References to LAST STEP</u>

Pg. 105T (Pg. 113T SE) - "I have said that the last step in the reawakening of knowledge is taken by God. This is true, but it is hard to explain in words because words are symbols, and nothing that is true need be explained. However, the Holy Spirit has the task of translating the useless into the useful, the meaningless into the meaningful, and the temporary into the timeless. He can therefore tell you something about this last step. God does not take steps, because His accomplishments are not gradual."

Pg. 199T (Pg. 214T SE) - "And then your Father will lean down to you and take the last step for you, by raising you unto Himself."

Pg. 99WB (Pg. 100WB SE) - "God does not forgive because He has never condemned. The blameless cannot blame, and those who have accepted their innocence see nothing to forgive. Yet forgiveness is the means by which I will recognize my innocence. It is the reflection of God's Love on earth. It will bring me near enough to Heaven that the Love of God can reach down to me and raise me up to Him."

LEVELS, ONE AND TWO

A Course in Miracles is written on two distinct levels. The text does not refer to them as such, and both are used, sometimes in the same sentence.

Anything that changes, or has an opposite, is what the *Course* refers to as Level Two. This includes forgiveness, because you can choose not to forgive, although it is the only thing in Level Two (i.e. world and body that is God-like, with the same properties as God.)

Level One refers to God and His creation (i.e. Sonship). This would contain only the unchangeable and eternal.

The cause and effect principle clearly points out the difference in the two levels. Level One --- God is the Cause and the Son (Sonship), is the Effect. Level Two --- Our thoughts are the cause and the world or body is the effect.

Now let's take a look at Level Two; here the statements are practical and by working on these levels we shall ultimately reach Level One, which is our oneness with God. In my opinion, Level Two is a level on which most of the *Course* is written. Here we deal with our thoughts, and through forgiveness we are shown which voice to heed.

ACIM References to LEVELS, ONE AND TWO

Pg. 20T (Pg. 23T SE) - "The body is merely part of your experience in the physical world, Its abilities can be and frequently are overevaluated. However, it is almost impossible to deny its existence in this world. Those who do so are engaging in a particularly unworthy form of denial."

Pg. 139T (Pg. 150T SE) - "Truth can only be experienced. It cannot be described and it cannot be explained. I can make you aware of the conditions of truth, but the experience is of God. Together we can meet its conditions, but truth will dawn upon you of itself."

Pg. 428T (Pg. 460T SE) - "The body does not separate you from your brother, and if you think it does you are insane.

LOVE: Heart of God

Throughout the *Course* the word Love is used to represent God. On Level One, God is omnipresent, and nothing else exists. Therefore, we are one with our Creator and have never left home.

On Level Two, the practical application of the *Course* talks about love between brothers. This is accomplished through forgiveness. In this type of love, we are not special, and love everyone equally. The vast majority of people taking the course say this type of love is not possible in the ego world. That belief is correct, but in the real world, it is.

The ego's point of view of love is ambivalent love, meaning simultaneously conflicting feelings. This means we love and hate at the same time. Bring it even more up to date, and it would be called conditional love, or co-dependent love. This means that I love you if you do certain things for me; if you stop doing those things, I no longer love you but hate you.

ACIM References to LOVE

Pg. 55T (Pg. 61T SE) - "No love in this world is without this ambivalence, and since no ego has experienced love without ambivalence the concept is beyond its understanding."

Pg. 247T (Pg. 265T SE) - "You cannot enter into real relationships with any of God's Sons unless you love them all and equally. Love is not special. If you single out part of the Sonship for your love, you are imposing guilt on all your relationships and making them unreal. You can love only as God loves. Seek not to love unlike Him, for there is no love apart from His. Until you recognize that this is true, you will have no idea what love is like."

Pg. 225WB (Pg. 230WB SE) - Perhaps you think that different kinds of love are possible. Perhaps you think there is a kind of love for this, a kind for that; a way of loving one, another way of loving still another. Love is one. It has no separate parts and no degrees; no kinds nor levels, no divergencies and

LOVE CONT'D

ACIM Reference to LOVE Cont'd

Pg. 225WB (Pg. 230WB SE) Cont'd - no distinctions. It is like itself, unchanged throughout. It never alters with a person or a circumstance. It is the Heart of God, and also of His Son. . . . No law the world obeys can help you grasp love's meaning. What the world believes was made to hide love's meaning, and to keep it dark and secret. There is not one principle the world upholds but violates the truth of what love is, and what you are as well. Seek not within the world to find your Self."

MAGIC

Magic is the attempt to solve a given problem at the effect level. The ego tells you the problem is in the world, or body, and that is where it needs solving. This works nicely for the ego because the problem involves a change in somebody or some circumstance.

In believing the problem is external and not in your mind, where the problem really exists, the ego seeks a magical solution by external remedies. If, for example, you have a headache, the ego says the problem is in your body and offers you a magical solution, aspirin. The *Course* is not against magic; it just says magic will not solve the problem at the source. You can take the aspirin and cure your headache, but the cause of the headache (tension, anger, separation, resentment, etc.) has not been cured; another headache or some type of discomfort will manifest itself again in the body.

Applying this to relationships, if you are angry, upset, etc. at another person, you can seek to disassociate yourself from him, but that does not solve the problem. You take yourself, which is the problem, with you. No matter where you go, there you are.

In a special relationship, you say that the other person is the one who can make us happy. Notice that magic always involves something on the outside.

ACIM References to MAGIC

Pg. 19T (Pg. 23T SE) - "We have referred to miracles as the means of correcting level confusion, for all mistakes must be corrected at the level on which they occur. Only the mind is capable of error. The body can act wrongly only when it is responding to misthought. The body cannot create, and the belief that it can, a fundamental error, produces all physical symptoms. Physical illness represents a belief in magic. The whole distortion that made magic rests on the belief that there is a creative ability in matter which the mind cannot control."

Pg. 20T (Pg. 24T SE) - "The value of the Atonement does not lie in the manner in which it is expressed. In fact, if it is used truly, it will inevitably be expressed in whatever way is most helpful to the receiver. This means that

MAGIC CONT'D

ACIM References to MAGIC Cont'd

Pg. 20T (Pg. 24T SE) cont'd - a miracle, to attain its full efficacy, must be expressed in a language that the recipient can understand without fear. This does not necessarily mean that this is the highest level of communication of which he is capable. It does mean, however, that it is the highest level of communication of which he is capable *now*."

MAKE: Miscreate, Miscreation

Make refers to the ego. The ego tells us we are incomplete, so we have to make something to fill in the gap, thereby making us complete. *Make* also refers to the attributes we give our brother, other than the role the Holy Spirit assigned to him.

On Level One, we made the ego out of our thought of being separated from God.

ACIM References to MAKE

Pg. 37T (Pg. 41T SE) - "If you attack error in another, you will hurt yourself. You cannot know your brother when you attack him. Attack is always made upon a stranger. You are making him a stranger by misperceiving him, and so you cannot know him. It is because you have made him a stranger that you are afraid of him."

Pg. 39T (Pg. 44T SE) - "When you make something, you do so out of a specific sense of lack or need. Anything made for a specific purpose has no true generalizability. When you make something to fill a perceived lack, you are tacitly implying that you believe in separation."

MIND: Mind of God

When the *Course* uses the word *Mind* with a capital "M", it is referring to the Mind of God. When it uses it with a small "m", it refers to the split mind. The split mind came about when we believed we separated from God. It does not refer to the brain, as the brain is in the physical realm, being a physical organ.

ACIM References to MIND

Pg. 19T (Pg. 23T SE) - "Only the mind is capable of error. The body can act wrongly only when it is responding to misthought."

Pg. 115T (Pg. 124T SE) - "The mind can, however, make up illusions, and if it does so it will believe in them, because that is how it made them."

Pg. 134T (Pg. 144T SE) - "Your mind is the means by which you determine your own condition, because mind is the mechanism of decision."

Pg. 92WB (Pg. 93WB SE) - "In my own mind, behind all my insane thoughts of separation and attack, is the knowledge that all is one forever. I have not lost the knowledge of who I am because I have forgotten it. It has been kept for me in the Mind of God, Who has not left His Thoughts. And I, who am among them, as one with them and one with Him."

MIRACLES

In the world of perception, or choice, a miracle is simply the right answer. It is also the love behind the choice for correction. It is not a parting of the seas, or any type of miraculous healing at the form level.

What we must always keep in mind is, "This is a course in cause and not effect."

Therefore, a miracle is the correct choice within our mind (cause). Hopefully, by making the correct choice it will be manifested in the form (body, world). This is not always the case. Miracle #35, "Miracles are expressions of love, but they may not have observable effects." This process undoes separation because we join with the Holy Spirit.

ACIM References to MIRACLES

Pg. 9T (Pg. 11T SE) - "The miracle joins in the Atonement by placing the mind in the service of the Holy Spirit. . . . The miracle is much like the body in that both are learning aids for facilitating a state in which they become unnecessary."

Pg. 10T (Pg. 13T SE) - "The miracle is a sign that the mind has chosen to be led by me in Christ's service."

Pg. 214T (Pg. 230T SE) - "The Holy Spirit is invisible, but you can see the results of His Presence, and through them you will learn that He is there. What He enables you to do is clearly not of this world, for miracles violate every law of reality as this world judges it. Every law of time and space, of magnitude and mass is transcended, for what the Holy Spirit enables you to do is clearly beyond all of them. Perceiving His results, you will understand where He must be, and finally know what He is."

Pg. 275T (Pg. 295T SE) - "The miracle is the recognition that this is true. Where there is love, your brother must give it to you because of what it is. But where there is a call for love, you must give it because of what you are."

Pg. 277T (Pg. 298T SE) - "You cannot be your guide to miracles, for it is you who made them necessary. . . . The miracle acknowledges His changlessness by seeing His Son as he always was, and not as he would make himself."

MIRACLES CONT'D

ACIM References to MIRACLES Cont'd

Pg. 137WB (Pg. 139WB SE) - "Perhaps it is not yet quite clear to you that each decision that you make is one between a grievance and a miracle. Each grievance stands like a dark shield of hate before the miracle it would conceal. And as you raise it up before your eyes, you will not see the miracle beyond. Yet all the while it waits for you in light, but you be-hold your grievances instead."

Pg. 463WB (Pg. 473WB SE) - "A miracle is a correction. It does not create, nor really change at all."

NEUTRAL

Neutral refers strictly to the world, things in the world, and the body. The Holy Spirit wants you to take the things the ego makes to separate (world, body, objects, etc.) and give them a different meaning. Their meaning then becomes one of joining, accomplished through forgiveness. He does this because form is the effect of our thoughts and can be given a different meaning. The mind determines the purpose given to form.

ACIM References to NEUTRAL

Pg. 547T (Pg. 589T SE) - "And like all the things you made, it can be used to serve another purpose, and to be the means for something else. It can be used to heal and not to hurt, if you so wish it be."

ONE-MINDEDNESS: Mind of God, Mind of Christ

One-mindedness has nothing to do with the world of perception (choice). It is the Mind of God, the pre-separation state where only knowledge exists.

ACIM References to ONE-MINDEDNESS

Pg. 53T (Pg. 59T SE) - "Salvation is nothing more than 'right-mindedness', which is not the One-mindedness of the Holy Spirit, but which must be achieved before One-mindedness is restored. Right-mindedness leads to the next step automatically, because right perception is uniformly without attack, and therefore wrong-mindedness is obliterated."

PERCEPTION

Perception (choice) is an internal thought, therefore, it comes from our mind and not the external world. Perception can be made with the Holy Spirit (right-mindedness), or with the ego (wrong-mindedness). This choice determines how we will see the external world.

Perception is only used in the world of choice, therefore this would strictly be Level Two. Perception (choice) from this level means everything we see we make a decision to join or separate. We make this decision with our split mind. (right or wrong-mindedness). There are no exceptions to this rule. Upon listening to the Holy Spirit, we see everyone as expressing love or crying for help. If we are listening to the ego; we perceive him as our enemy.

ACIM References to PERCEPTION

Pg. 487T (Pg. 524T SE) - "Perception rests on choosing; knowledge does not."

Pg. 489T (Pg 526T SE) - "Perception's basic law could thus be said, 'You will rejoice at what you see because you see it to rejoice.' And while you think that suffering and sin will bring you joy, so long will they be there for you to see."

Pg. 67WB (Pg. 67WB SE) - "Perception is not an attribute of God. His is the realm of knowledge. Yet He has created the Holy Spirit as the Mediator between perception and knowledge. Without this link with God, perception would have replaced knowledge forever in your mind. With this link with God, percep-tion will become so changed and purified that it will lead to knowledge. That is its function as the Holy Spirit sees it. Therefore, that is its function in truth."

PROJECT: Projection, Displacement

This is the second, and most frequently used weapon at the ego's disposal. Since we feel guilty at the core of our being, we must experience guilt. Level One projection is the original thought of separation projected outward.

Having this guilt (i.e., anger, attack thoughts, feelings of inadequacy, feeling guilty for not being good enough, etc.) we want to get rid of the guilt. Now, inasmuch as there are only two voices to whom we can listen, Holy Spirit or the ego, God becomes the enemy in the ego's thought system, and we go to the ego for help. The ego says, "I can get rid of your guilt for you." The process it offers for getting rid of our guilt is to throw it or hurl it onto somebody else. This is known as projection. And now the ego says, "I have gotten rid of the guilt for you." Having *given away* our guilt, we now have somebody or something else on which to blame it on. Again see how nicely the ego keeps the problem away from the answer.

ACIM References to PROJECT

Pg. 89T (Pg. 96T SE) - "Projection and attack are inevitably related, because projection is always a means of justifying attack. Anger without projection is impossible."

Pg. 91T (Pg. 98T SE) - "The ego projects to exclude, and therefore to deceive."

Pg. 223T (Pg. 239T SE) - "The ultimate purpose of projection is always to get rid of guilt. . . . Yet consider how strange a solution the ego's arrangement is. You project guilt to get rid of it, but you are actually merely concealing it. You do experience the guilt, but you have no idea why."

62

REAL WORLD

The real world is a state of mind, brought about through complete forgiveness, that replaces the ego's world. The purpose the ego places on the world is one of projecting guilt.

Upon choosing the Holy Spirit to be your guide, you undo the thought of separation and see the happy dream, which is the vision of Christ. It is the mind that changes its perception; the world remains the same. Therefore, what remains is only our loving thoughts and this is the real world.

ACIM References to REAL WORLD

Pg. 216T (Pg. 232T SE) - "Through the eyes of Christ, only the real world exists and only the real world can be seen. As you decide so will you see. And all that you see but witnesses to your decision."

Pg. 328T (Pg. 352T SE) - "Can you imagine how beautiful those you forgive will look to you? In no fantasy have you ever seen anything so lovely, Nothing you see here, sleeping or waking, comes near to such loveliness. And nothing will you value like unto this, nor hold so dear. Nothing that you remember that made your heart sing with joy has ever brought you even a little part of the happiness this sight will bring you. For you will see the Son of God. You will behold the beauty the Holy Spirit loves to look upon, and which He thanks the Father for. He was created to see this for you, until you learned to see it for yourself. And all His teaching leads to seeing it and giving thanks with Him. . . . This loveliness is not a fantasy. It is the real world, bright and clean and new, with everything sparkling under the open sun."

Pg. 590T (Pg. 635T SE) - "The real world is the state of mind in which the only purpose of the world is seen to be forgiveness."

Pg. 591T (Pg. 636T SE) - "The real world is a state in which the mind has learned how easily do idols go when they are still perceived but wanted not."

REVELATION

Revelation is the pre-separation state where God and His Son are in constant communication. Brief return of this state can be experienced in the Holy Instant.

ACIM References to REVELATION

Pg. 3T (Pg. 5T SE) - "Miracles are a way of earning release from fear. Revelation induces a state in which fear has already been abolished. Miracles are thus a means and revelation is an end."

Pg. 4T (Pg. 7T SE) - "Revelation induces complete but temporary suspension of doubt and fear. It reflects the original form of communication between God and His creations."

Pg. 5T (Pg. 7T SE) - "Revelation is intensely personal and cannot be meaningfully translated. That is why any attempt to describe it in words is impossible. Revelation induces only experience. Miracles, on the other hand, induce action."

<u>RIGHT-MINDED</u>: Miracle minded, Right-mindedness

Right-mindedness is the part of our split mind that listens to the Holy Spirit. This is the voice for forgiveness. Choosing His guidance leads us to One-mindedness.

ACIM References to RIGHT-MINDED

Pg. 24T (Pg. 27T SE) - "Only right-mindedness can correct in a way that has any real effect."

Pg. 38T (Pg. 42T SE) - "Right-mindedness is not to be confused with the knowing mind, because it is applicable only to right perception."

Pg. 75MT (Pg. 79MT SE) - "The mind can be right or wrong, depending on the voice to which it listens. *Right-mindedness* listens to the Holy Spirit, forgives the world, and through Christ's vision sees the real world in its place."

SACRIFICE

Sacrifice is at the bedrock of the ego's thought system. This is the belief that someone must lose for someone to gain. In this system of thought you feel you have to give up (pay) something to receive something. On a deeper level, we feel we must pay a price (suffering, atoning and doing good deeds) to receive God's Love, because we believe we have separated from Him.

The reversal of this principle comes from the Holy Spirit. He tells us that we are already complete and that whatever we give away increases in our life. As the Course says, "Ideas leave not their source." Keep in mind that things (effect, form) first start in our minds (cause). In this process (forgiveness) everyone gains.

ACIM References to SACRIFICE

Pg. 33T (Pg. 37T SE) - "Sacrifice is a notion totally unknown to God. . . . Innocence is incapable of sacrificing anything, because the innocent mind has everything and strives only to protect its wholeness. It cannot project."

Pg. 302T (Pg. 325T SE) - "Sacrifice is so essential to your thought system that salvation apart from sacrifice means nothing to you. Your confusion of sacrifice and love is so profound that you cannot conceive of love without sacrifice. And it is this that you must look upon; sacrifice is attack, not love. If you would accept but this one idea, your fear of love would vanish. Guilt cannot last when the idea of sacrifice has been removed. For if there is sacrifice, someone must pay and someone must get. And the only question that remains is how much is the price, and for getting what?"

Pg. 504T (Pg. 542T SE) - "In the 'dynamics' of attack is sacrifice a key idea. It is the pivot upon which all compromise, all desperate attempts to strike a bargain, and all conflicts achieve a seeming balance. It is the symbol of the central theme that *somebody must lose*. Its focus on the body is apparent for it is always an attempt to limit loss. The body is itself a sacrifice; a giving up of power in the name of saving just a little for yourself. To see a brother in another body, separate from yours, is the expression of a wish to see a little part of him and sacrifice the rest. Look at the world and you will see nothing attached to anything beyond itself. All seeming entities can come a little nearer, or go a little farther off, but cannot join. The world you see is based on "sacrifice" of oneness. It is a picture of complete disunity and total lack of joining."

SCARCITY PRINCIPLE

This belief forms the basis of the ego's thought system. It implies we are lacking; therefore, we seek in the world (form) things to make us complete (i.e. special relationships, idols, food, drugs, power, etc.). I have included food, drugs and power, but the *Course* always refers to relationships. These objects, which we use to fill ourselves, the *Course* refers to as idols.

The Course constantly substitutes the scarcity principle with the word "sacrifice." Because we believe that in order to get something we must give something."

ACIM References to SCARCITY PRINCIPLE

Pg. 52T (Pg. 58T SE) - "Only those who have a real and lasting sense of abundance can be truly charitable. This is obvious when you consider what is involved. To the ego, to give anything implies that you will have to do without it. When you associate giving with sacrifice, you give only because you believe that you are somehow getting something better, and can therefore do without the thing you give. 'Giving to get' is an inescapable law of the ego, which always evaluates itself in relation to other egos. It is therefore continually preoccupied with the belief in scarcity that gave rise to it."

SECOND COMING

The Second Coming has nothing to do with the physical incarnation of Jesus Christ. It is simply the return of our awareness as the Son of God.

ACIM References to SECOND COMING

Pg. 58T (Pg. 64T SE) - "The First Coming of Christ is merely another name for the creation, for Christ is the Son of God. The Second Coming of Christ means nothing more than the end of the ego's rule and the healing of the mind."

Pg. 159T (Pg. 170T SE) - "The Second Coming is the awareness of reality, not its return."

Pg. 439WB (Pg. 449WB SE) - Christ's Second Coming, which is sure as God, is merely the correction of mistakes, and the return of sanity. It is a part of the condition that restores the never lost, and reestablishes what is forever and forever true. It is the invitation to God's Word to take illusion's place; the willingness to let forgiveness rest upon all things without exception and without reserve."

SELF

Self, with a capital "S", always refers to the Son of God, which is synonymous with Christ. This part of you is in constant communication with your Creator because of your Oneness with Him.

When referring to the ego, the word "self" will have a small "s".

ACIM References to SELF

Pg. 620T (Pg. 667T SE) - "His strength is yours because He is the Self That God created as His only Son."

Pg. 114WB (Pg. 115WB SE) - "You who were created by Love like Itself can hold no grievances and know your Self. To hold a grievance is to forget who you are. To hold a grievance is to see yourself as a body. To hold a grievance is to let the ego rule your mind and to condemn the body to death. Perhaps you do not yet fully realize just what holding grievances does to your mind. It seems to split you off from your Source and make you unlike Him. It makes you believe that He is like what you think you have become, for no one can conceive of his Creator as unlike himself."

Pg. 162WB (Pg. 164WB SE) - "*I am as God created me. I am His Son eternally.* Now try to reach the Son of God in you. This is the Self That never sinned, nor made an image to replace reality. This is the Self That never left Its home in God to walk the world uncertainly. This is the Self That knows no fear, nor could conceive of loss or suffering or death."

Pg. 167WB (Pg. 169WB SE) - "The self you made can never be your Self, nor can your Self be split in two, and still be what It is and must forever be."

SEPARATION: Gap, Dissociation, Separate, Separate will, Exclusion, Division, Delusion, Exclusion

Separation is spoken of on two distinct levels. Level One speaks of the thought of separation of God and His Son (Sonship). In eternity this never occurred, and the word "sin" may be substituted.

Level Two (world, body) is the belief we can separate from our brother. This is accomplished because we have a split (separate) mind.

ACIM References to SEPARATION

Pg. 88T (Pg. 96T SE) - "Any split in mind must involve a rejection of part of it, and this is the belief in separation. The wholeness of God, which is His peace, cannot be appreciated except by a whole mind that recognizes the wholeness of God's creation. By this recognition it knows its Creator. Exclusion and separation are synonymous, as are separation and dissociation."

Pg. 220T (Pg. 236T SE) - "If you did not feel guilty you could not attack, for condemnation is the root of attack. It is the judgment of one mind by another as unworthy of love and deserving of punishment. But herein lies the split. For the mind that judges perceives itself as separate from the mind being judged."

Pg. 320T (Pg. 344T SE) - "Separation is only the decision *not* to know yourself."

Pg. 552T (Pg. 594T SE) - "The separation started with the dream the Father was deprived of His Effects, and powerless to keep them since He was no longer their Creator."

Pg. 231WB (Pg. 237WB SE) - "Fear has made everything you think you see. All separation, all distinctions, and the multitude of differences you believe make up the world. They are not there. Love's enemy has made them up."

Pg. 43MT (Pg. 45MT SE) - "A magic thought, by its mere presence, acknowledges a separation from God."

SICKNESS: Separation

Sickness always involves a split or separation that has taken place in our mind, and then projected onto our body. The ego manages to focus our mind on the body (effect) and away from the mind (cause). All sickness comes from holding onto unforgiving thoughts.

On the form level, we get sick for countless reasons to show someone how much he has hurt us, to make people feel sorry for us (therefore, to receive sympathy), a flu bug in the air, etc., all of which is merely a blanket over an unforgiving thought. Note: The Course is not saying there aren't flu bugs in the air; it is just saying that they are not the cause of sickness.

ACIM References to SICKNESS

Pg. 144T (Pg. 155T SE) - "The body's condition lies solely in your interpretation of its function."

Pg. 145T (Pg. 156T SE) - "Sickness is merely another example of your insistence on asking guidance of a teacher who does not know the answer."

Pg.146T (Pg. 157T SE) - "When the ego tempts you to sickness do not ask the Holy Spirit to heal the body, for this would merely be to accept the ego's belief that the body is the proper aim of healing. Ask, rather, that the Holy Spirit teach you the right *perception* of the body, for perception alone can be distorted. Only perception can be sick, because only perception can be wrong. . . . Wholeness heals because it is of the mind. All forms of sickness, even unto death, are physical expressions of the fear of awakening."

Pg. 173T (Pg. 185T SE) - "If God created you perfect, you *are* perfect. If you believe you can be sick, you have placed other gods before Him."

Pg. 514T (Pg. 553T SE) - "All sickness comes from separation. When the separation is denied, it goes. For it is gone as soon as the idea that brought it has been healed, and been replaced by sanity."

ACIM References to SICKNESS Cont'd

Pg. 553T (Pg. 595T SE) - "The miracle is useless if you learn but that the body can be healed, for this is not the lesson it was sent to teach. The lesson is the *mind* was sick that thought the body could be sick; projecting out its guilt caused no-thing, and had no effects."

Pg. 554T (Pg. 597T SE) - "The cause of pain is separation, not the body, which is only its effect."

Pg. 560T (Pg. 603T SE) - "Sickness is anger taken out upon the body, so that it will suffer pain."

SIN: Mistake, Error

The ego's version of sin would be the belief of our separation from God. In the ego's belief system, this actually occurred. Actually, we can't commit sin and have not separated from God. All we can do is make mistakes. Mistakes need correction, not punishment. So, when mistakes, which are correctable, occur, all we have to do is choose once again. (Choose Holy Spirit instead of the ego.) We do not have to suffer for our mistakes unless we believe we need to suffer.

ACIM References to SIN

Pg. 374T (Pg. 402T SE) - "It is essential that error be not confused with sin, and it is this distinction that makes salvation possible. For error can be corrected, and the wrong made right. But sin, were it possible, would be irreversible."

Pg. 442T (Pg. 475T SE) - "And yet mistakes, regardless of their form, can be corrected."

Pg. 515T (Pg. 555T SE) - "Sin is not error, for it goes beyond correction to impossibility. Yet the belief that it is real has made some errors seem forever past the hope of healing, and the lasting grounds for hell."

Pg. 529T (Pg. 569T SE) - "Sins are beyond forgiveness just because they would entail effects that cannot be undone and overlooked entirely. In their undoing lies the proof that they are merely errors. Let yourself be healed that you may be forgiving, offering salvation to your brother and yourself."

SPECIAL: Specialness

Specialness, from the ego's point of view, means we are lacking, not complete; being incomplete we feel a need for completion. The ego tells us to seek our completion in the world (other people, drugs, power, etc.).

Note: The *Course*, most of the time, deals strictly with our relationship with people.

The world itself fosters differences, which is exactly what the ego wants us to see. If there are differences, we have to judge; since we have judged, there must be condemnation and attack (which comes from our projection of guilt).

The Holy Spirit tells us we are lacking and what we need is God. Having united with our Creator, we can now form relationships not out of need but with a genuine sharing.

ACIM References to SPECIAL

PG. 293T (Pg. 314T SE) - "You have so little faith in yourself because you are unwilling to accept the fact that perfect love is in you. And so you seek without for what you cannot find without."

Pg. 586T (Pg. 631T SE) - "Behind the search for every idol lies the yearning for completion. Wholeness has no form because it is unlimited. To seek a special person or a thing to add to you to make yourself complete, can only mean that you believe some form is missing. And by finding this, you will achieve completion in a form you like. This is the purpose of an idol; that you will not look beyond it, to the source of the belief that you are incomplete. Only if you had sinned could this be so. For sin is the idea you are alone and separated off from what is whole. And thus it would be necessary for the search for wholeness to be made beyond the boundaries of limits on yourself."

.

SPIRIT

Spirit is the nature of our true reality, that of our oneness with God. It is changeless and eternal, in stark contrast to the body.

ACIM References to SPIRIT

Pg. 614T (Pg. 660T SE) - "You see the flesh or recognize the spirit. There is no compromise between the two. If one is real the other must be false, for what is real denies its opposite. There is no choice in vision but this one. What you decide in this determines all you see and think is real and hold as true. On this one choice does all your world depend, for here have you established what you are, as flesh or spirit in your own belief. If you choose flesh, you never will escape the body as your own reality, for you have chosen that you want it so. But choose the spirit, and all Heaven bends to touch your eyes and bless your holy sight, that you may see the world of flesh no more except to heal and comfort and to bless."

Pg. 167WB (Pg. 169WB SE) - "Spirit makes use of mind as means to find its Self-expression. And the mind which serves the spirit is at peace and filled with joy. Its power comes from spirit, and it is fulfilling happily its function here. Yet mind can also see itself divorced from spirit, and perceive itself within a body it confuses with itself. Without its function then it has no peace, and happiness is alien to its thoughts."

SUBCONSCIOUS

In truth, there is no subconscious, i.e., the place into which we supposedly push our feelings. The subconscious is the *secret place* where we unload our fear by suppressing (denying) it and then removing it from our awareness by the process of projection. In our horror at looking at our guilt, our ego (fear) says, "Let's not look at this awful thing in our mind." (Remember, we are afraid to look within because God is there, and since we believe we separated from Him, we are afraid of His retaliation.) So, being afraid to look at our own fear, we constantly go to the ego for help. He uses his most potent weapon, i.e., denial.

Keep in mind that nothing happens by accident and everything happens to us by our choice. But after we project our fear, we magically forget we did so and wonder why this happened to us. Because our ego has dropped the veil of forgetfulness (or denial) over our mind, the memory of the decision we actually made of our own free will is now obscured.

SUFFERING

Suffering is one of the foundations of the ego's thought system. It stems from the belief we separated from God, and God will punish us for this act.

The ego state we have to suffer for our *sins* and deserve punishment because of our guilt. If sin were possible, this would be the case. Since sin is impossible, the *Course* states we only make mistakes. Mistakes and errors need correction, not punishment. Upon making a mistake, the *Course* says for us to say: "Choose once again." This means choose the Holy Spirit this time instead of the ego.

ACIM Reference to SUFFERING

PG. 179WB (pg. 182WB SE) - "Today we will continue with the theme of happiness. This is a key idea in understanding what salvation means. You still believe it asks for suffering as penance for your 'sins.' This is not so. Yet you must think it so while you believe that sin is real, and that God's Son can sin."

TEACHER OF GOD: Miracle worker, Messenger, Minister of God

A teacher of God, as stated in the *Course*, does not necessarily mean a teacher of the *Course*. Although in one section it points out that to become a teacher of God, you have to have completed the Workbook. This means to be a *teacher of God* in the *Course*, you have to have completed the Workbook.

What this means is that most of the time when you choose forgiveness instead of the ego, you become a teacher of God. It also makes it clear that you are teaching all the time; it is just a matter of choosing what you want to teach.

ACIM References to TEACHER OF GOD

Pg. 22T (Pg. 25T SE) - "The healer who relies on his owns readiness is endangering his understanding. You are perfectly safe as long as you are completely unconcerned about your readiness, but maintain a consistent trust in mine."

Pg. 278T (Pg. 299T SE) - "If you want peace you must abandon the teacher of attack. The Teacher of peace will never abandon you."

Pg. 1MT (Pg. 1MT SE) - "The question is not whether you will teach, for in that there is not choice. The purpose of the course might be said to provide you with a means of choosing what you want to teach on the basis of what you want to learn. You cannot give to someone else, but only to yourself and this you learn through teaching."

Pg. 3MT (Pg. 3MT SE) - "A teacher of God is anyone who chooses to be one."

Pg. 18MT (Pg. 19MT SE) - "They stand for the Alternative. With God's Word in their minds they come in benediction, not to heal the sick but to remind them of the remedy God has already given them."

VISION

Vision is using the perception of the Holy Spirit (versus the ego), whereby you look past the body to the Christ (Light) within your brother. Vision is solely of the mind (internal) whereby you join with your brother. Vision has absolutely nothing to do with our physical sight.

ACIM References to VISION

Pg. 47WB (Pg. 47WB SE) - "The idea for today is the springboard for vision. From this idea will the world open up before you, and you will look upon it and see in it what you have never seen before. Nor will what you saw before be even faintly visible to you. Today we are trying to use a new kind of 'projection.' We are not attempting to get rid of what we do not like by seeing it outside. Instead, we are trying to see in the world what is in our minds, and what we want to recognize is there. Thus, we are trying to join with what we see, rather than keeping it apart from us. That is the fundamental difference between vision and the way you see."

Pg. 292WB (Pg. 299WB SE) - "Christ's vision has one law. It does not look upon a body, and mistake it for the Son whom God created. It beholds a light beyond the body; an idea beyond what can be touched, a purity undimmed by errors, pitiful mistakes, and fearful thoughts of guilt from dreams of sin. It sees no separation. And it looks on everyone, on every circumstance, all happenings and all events, without the slightest fading of the light it sees. This can be taught; and must be taught by all who would achieve it. It requires but the recognition that the world can not give anything that faintly can compare with this in value; nor set up a goal that does not merely disappear when this has been perceived. And this you give today: See no one as a body. Greet him as the Son of God he is, acknowledging that he is one with you in holiness."

WORLD

The world came into existence the instant the thought of sin appeared in the Son of God. The world and body are the effect of this one thought (which gave rise to the ego) projected outward. The world, created from the thought of separation, therefore, has nothing to do with the Oneness of God. Look at the world of the ego. Everything in it points to separation, difference, big and small. This reinforces our belief in sin and guilt, leading us further and further away from our Creator.

The Holy Spirit's use of the world is a place where we come to learn our lessons in forgiveness through the Holy Spirit. He teaches us the world is neutral, neither good nor bad. Its only purpose is the one we give it. It is just the effect (form); our mind is the cause. Upon changing our mind, the purpose we give the world can be changed.

ACIM References to WORLD

Pg. 34WB   (Pg. 34WB SE) - "Every thought you have makes up some segment of the world you see. It is with your thoughts, then, that we must work, if your perception of the world is to be changed. If the cause of the world you see is attack thoughts, you must learn that it is these thoughts which you do not want. There is no point in lamenting the world. There is no point in trying to change the world. It is incapable of change because it is merely an effect. But there is indeed a point in changing your thoughts about the world. Here you are changing the cause. The effect will change automatically."

Pg. 125WB   (Pg. 127WB SE) - "Your picture of the world can only mirror what is within."

Pg. 35MT   (Pg. 36MT SE) - "Until forgiveness is complete, the world does have a purpose. It becomes the home in which forgiveness is born, and where it grows and becomes stronger and more all-embracing. Here is it nourished, for here it is needed."

WRONG-MINDEDNESS

Wrong-mindedness is the portion of our mind that listens to the voice of the ego.

ACIM References to WRONG-MINDEDNESS

Pg. 37T (Pg. 42T SE) - "The ego is a wrong-minded attempt to perceive yourself as you wish to be, rather than as you are."

Pg. 75MT (Pg. 79MT SE) - "*Wrong-mindedness* listens to the ego and makes illusions; perceiving sin and justifying anger, and seeing guilt, disease and death as real."

To obtain additional copies write to:
Gene Skaggs Jr.
1140 Riverwood Drive
Nashville, TN   37216
Telephone: (615) 262-5044
Retail: $10 (Includes postage & handling)
or contact your nearest bookstore.
ISBN: 0-9633394-0-0